DARREN SHAN

HAGUROSAN

With illustrations by
ZACK MCLAUGHLIN

For:
the spirits of Hagurosan mountain in Japan
– thank you for giving me this story.

First published in 2013 in Great Britain by
Barrington Stoke Ltd
18 Walker Street, Edinburgh, EH3 7LP

www.barringtonstoke.co.uk

Adapted from a story originally published in
Kids' Night In, Harper Collins, 2003

ISBN: 978-1-78112-206-8

Printed in China by Leo

CONTENTS

No path is ordinary
All are magical
Winding their ways to wonders

Chapter 1

The Boy and the Cake

"I don't want to go to the shrine," said Hagurosan. "I want to play."

"There will be time to play later," his mother told him. She handed him a small cake she had just baked. "Take this and offer it to the spirits."

"But – " Hagurosan began.

His mother sighed. "Please," she said. "I am too tired to argue."

And because Hagurosan was a good child,
he pulled a face, stuck the cake in his pocket,
and set off on the hour-long walk to the shrine.

The sun sizzled in the sky. Children played in the dust, splashing each other with water from the well. Some of Hagurosan's friends saw him. "Come and play with us!" they called. But Hagurosan shook his head and walked on.

Hagurosan climbed the small hill above his village. At the top he stopped to admire the round huts and straw roofs. Then he trotted down the gentle slope to the base of the Holy Mountain, where the real climb began.

The gods lived on top of the cloud-capped mountain. The clouds were the floor of their home. When the sky was blue, it meant they were away.

Only priests climbed to the top of the Holy Mountain. It was guarded by snake-dogs, and they would kill any foolish human who disobeyed the holy law that banned them from the top.

Lower down the Mountain, there was a shrine where the spirits lived. Hagurosan wasn't quite sure about the ways in which spirits were different from gods, but he knew they weren't as powerful. They were also more involved with humans. Gods only helped with important matters, such as war, or diseases that threatened the land. The spirits, on the other hand, could protect a farmer's crops, or make sure a woman's birthing time went well.

The climb was hard. The path was lined with trees, but the sun still found its way between the leaves, and Hagurosan was soon sweating. He stopped by a stream to wash his face and drink. The stream was a wild torrent in winter, but today it was a weak trickle.

As Hagurosan rested, he saw a hungry bird turn over a pebble and peck at the insects below. Hagurosan's stomach rumbled. Many splendid fruits grew on the Holy Mountain, but all were forbidden to the villagers. Only the priests could harvest the crops here.

Hagurosan's right hand crept to his pocket. "I can't eat the cake," he muttered to himself. "Not all of it. But I'm sure the spirits won't mind if I take a small bite." He pulled out the cake and nibbled at a corner. Then he nibbled at the other corners, to make it look as though the cake had been baked with slanted corners in the first place. Pleased with this plan, he went to put the cake back in his pocket. But then, because he did not want to break it, he decided to keep it safe in his hand. He climbed on up the Holy Mountain.

Of course Hagurosan soon found that a cake in a boy's hand has a habit of finding its way to his lips. As he climbed, he nibbled – a bit here, a bit there. He meant to leave a large chunk, but by the time he reached the shrine, only crumbs remained. They stuck to his fingers like glittering brown stars. And so he licked them up before he entered the shrine, so that he could place clean hands together and pray.

All of us sin
But no sin can define us
If we set out to make it right

Chapter 2

The Shrine on the Mountain

Short stone statues stood dotted in a circle around the shrine. Inside, the statues were larger. The biggest was at the centre, twice Hagurosan's size. All of the statues had faces which were human and yet not human. Most had been covered in layers of clothing – a cape, a hat, a shawl. Toys lay at the feet of some statues, or tools, or coins. (There were not many coins. Hagurosan came from a poor village. They bartered with other villages for most of their goods.) Food – rotting cakes – surrounded every statue. All of these gifts had been left as offerings to the spirits.

Hagurosan's family always left their offerings at the feet of a statue near the back of the shrine. It had been built by Hagurosan's great-grandfather, and it was meant to look like him. But today Hagurosan did not dare face that statue. He had eaten the offering and it was only now, inside the shrine, that he understood the size of his sin. He had taken food meant for the spirits. People who did that were struck down dead or inflicted with a dreadful disease. Sometimes their families were cursed, too.

Hagurosan considered running away and lying to his mother, but he knew the spirits could not be tricked. His only hope was to throw himself at their mercy and pray that they took pity on him.

Hagurosan walked to the statue at the centre of the shrine. As he walked he prayed, with his head bent and his hands joined. When he reached the statue, he fell to his knees and prayed for several minutes. Only then did he look up at the weather-beaten face.

"I didn't mean to eat the cake," Hagurosan said. A tear trickled from his left eye. "I only wanted a bit of it. But I couldn't stop once I started." He rooted through his pockets, looking for something else to offer the spirits. But his pockets were empty. He could take off his shorts and leave them, but that would mean walking back to the village naked.

"Please don't curse me," Hagurosan sobbed. "If you forgive me, I'll come back with all my toys. I'll give you all my dinners for a week. Anything!"

A light breeze whistled through the trees, but that was the only response. Hagurosan stood up, not sure what to do next. "If you curse me," he said to the statue, "will you please not curse my family? They didn't eat the cake. That was just me."

Hagurosan turned and walked away, but before he made it out of the shrine, something twinkled on the ground and caught his eye. Stopping, he bent over and found a small silver coin nestled in a bed of moss.

Hagurosan's heart beat faster. A real silver coin! He'd never held one before. A copper coin, yes, a couple of times. But never silver. His head spun as he thought of all the things he could buy. Toys, sweet cakes, clothes. A present for his mother. She loved it when Hagurosan's

father returned from market with presents. It didn't happen very often, but when it did she smiled her widest smile and was in a good mood for days after.

Hagurosan gripped the coin tight, and started forward at a run ... then stopped.

He opened his hand and gazed down at the coin. Then he looked back at the tall statue in the centre of the shrine. Although Hagurosan knew it was impossible, he had the feeling that the statue's eyes had moved. They seemed to be focused on him now, judging him.

All things in life are hidden
Waiting to be uncovered
For the rest of time

Chapter 3

The Silver Coins

A handful of seconds passed.

"OK," Hagurosan sighed. He walked back to the statue and went down on his knees. With a heavy heart, he set the coin down on the floor in front of the statue. There weren't many other offerings here, but every one was impressive – a beautiful mirror, necklaces, a leather wallet, and several sparkling jewels. People left only the best gifts at this statue, when they had something extra special to wish for.

"There," Hagurosan said. "It's worth much more than the cake. You could buy a hundred cakes with it. But it's yours now. I don't deserve it."

He glanced up at the statue, hoping it would come to life, smile at him, and tell him that he could keep the coin. But the statue did not move. With one last sad look at the coin, Hagurosan rose. He was on his feet before he remembered that he hadn't made a wish. With so great a gift, Hagurosan should have been able to make an extra special wish. But maybe he didn't have the right to wish for anything. After all, the gift had been offered to make up for eating the cake. At the same time, it would be a shame to waste such a special wish if he could make one.

"I know," he said, as a wonderful idea came to him. "Bless the children of the world, especially those in need of help. Look after them and grant them happiness and a safe place to live. This is my wish."

Hagurosan bowed low to the statue, turned and walked towards the exit. But again, he stopped short. There was another coin! It lay in almost the same place, and looked very much like the first coin. Hagurosan felt faint. To find two silver coins in the same day was like something from a dream.

As Hagurosan picked up the coin, doubt entered his mind. Was this a gift from the spirits? Was it a reward for giving the other coin to them? Or was it just good luck? If it was luck, then he should give this coin to the spirits as well. He still felt guilty about the cake. If he took this coin, the guilt would grow inside him and eat him away just as he had eaten the cake.

"This has taught me a lesson I'll never forget," Hagurosan said, as he took the coin to the statue and dropped it beside the first coin. He still wished he could keep the coin, but he knew he was doing the right thing.

Hagurosan headed for the exit again, faster than before, eager to race down the Holy Mountain and tell his friends what had happened. But, for the third time that day, he stopped before he had set a foot outside the shrine.

There was *another* coin, nestled on its side in the moss!

This time Hagurosan didn't touch the coin. He stared at it, afraid. This wasn't normal. It wasn't just that he'd found three silver coins in the same spot on the same day. He had seen no sign of the second and third when he picked up the first.

Now Hagurosan searched the ground, scattering the moss, sweeping through the dirt, making sure there were no other coins. When he was satisfied that this was the final one, he took it to the statue, set it down next to the others and again went to leave.

There was another coin.

Hagurosan stood over the coin, shivering. He stared at it for what felt like a year. His stomach was tight with fear.

Then he stepped over it and hurried for the exit.

The voice we hear in our heart
Is the voice that says on Day One –
Form and be born

Chapter 4

A Pact

"**Wait**," said a voice that was all voices.

Hagurosan froze.

"**We do not want you to leave**," said the voice that was all voices.

Hagurosan managed to turn his head. He thought he would see the lips of the giant statue move, but they didn't. The lips did not move on any of the statues. But words came from them anyway.

"**We want you to collect the coins**," said the voice that was all voices. "**When the day comes** that you see no coin, you may leave with our blessing."

"Wh-wh-wh-what if I ... luh-luh-leave before that?" Hagurosan croaked.

"Then we cannot grant your wish," said the voice that was all voices, and after that it was silent.

*

Late that night, Hagurosan's father came looking for him. He found his son huddled on the ground in front of the shrine's largest statue, crying softly. "Hagurosan," he said, touching the boy's trembling back. "What is wrong?"

Hagurosan turned to his father and held him tight. "The spirits won't let me go!" he moaned. "I ate their cake and now they say I've got to stay here to make my wish come true. But I don't want it to come true – not if it means I can't go home!"

Hagurosan's father let the boy babble,
then worked the full story out of him. He was
worried by his son's tale. His first thought was
that Hagurosan had made it up. But he could
see the four silver coins lying together at the
statue's feet.

"Where did you find the coins?" Hagurosan's father asked. When Hagurosan showed him, he searched the ground over and over to make sure it was clear. "Now," he said, with a smile for his son. "You don't see any coins, do you?"

"No," Hagurosan sniffed.

"Then come with me." Hagurosan's father held his hands out.

Hagurosan took a step towards his father. A second. A third. Then he stopped, bent and picked up a dull silver coin. "See?" he said in a low voice. He turned and placed the coin in front of the statue with the others.

Hagurosan's father stared at his son in wonder, then spun round and ran down the Holy Mountain to fetch the local priest.

*

The priest did not believe the story at first, and he was angry at being disturbed during his

24

supper. But when he saw Hagurosan produce eight silver coins in a row, his anger gave way to wonder.

"It is a miracle," the priest said to Hagurosan's father and the small group of villagers who'd got wind that something strange was happening. "But I cannot make sense of it," he told them. "I will need to ask for the help of wiser priests than me."

"But it will take you several days to walk to any place with another priest," Hagurosan's father said. "What will my son do until then?"

"Stay here," the priest said. "And pick up the coins. As many as he can."

The priest left, sweeping down the Holy Mountain with his robes flapping around him. Hagurosan's father held a quick meeting with the other villagers. In the end they bundled their spare clothes together and passed them to Hagurosan. "You must sleep here," his father said.

"What about you?" Hagurosan asked. "Will you stay, too?"

"I cannot," his father said. "It is forbidden for normal people to spend the night here. But I will return in the morning and bring your mother."

Hagurosan's father hugged him hard, then left with the other villagers. Hagurosan felt very alone. He wished with all his heart to race after his father and the other men. But he didn't dare disobey the will of the spirits, so he pulled the clothes tight around his body and tried to rock himself to sleep.

When the first choice was made
Human souls were conceived
And the universe rejoiced

Chapter 5
A Choice

Hagurosan's mother marched up the Holy Mountain the next morning. She was determined to return to the village with her son. But when she saw him pick coins out of what seemed to be thin air, she realised her son was at the centre of something wonderful. Instead of taking Hagurosan from the shrine, she comforted him as best she could. She gave him biscuits, and promised to return later with fresh cakes and bread, fish and meat, or anything else he desired.

Over the next few days, the people in the village took turns to carry food up the Holy

Mountain to Hagurosan. They also brought him clothes and toys. Many children came to play with him. They were odd with him at first, since they had heard their parents talk of him as a boy marvel. But after a few minutes they saw that he was the same Hagurosan as always, and played with him just like before.

When he wasn't playing with his friends,
Hagurosan picked up coins. He lost count of
the number in the middle of the second day,
but the pile was soon as high as his knees. The
villagers said he must have picked up five or six
hundred coins – a fortune.

Each time Hagurosan found a coin, he
prayed that it would be the last. But every time
he tried to leave, a new coin was waiting to be
added to the pile that grew and grew at the
foot of the statue.

Twelve days later, the village priest returned with seven older, wiser priests by his side. The villagers had never seen so many priests before, or such important ones. Most were scared of them and stayed inside their huts. They were afraid that the priests might think that Hagurosan's coins were a bad omen, and perhaps curse the whole village.

Some braver visitors stayed by the shrine. The village priest told these people to go. Then the seven senior priests entered the shrine and stood in a large circle around Hagurosan. They made Hagurosan show them his ability to find the magical coins. Then they tried and failed to do the same. Once this was over, they questioned Hagurosan for hours. Some shouted at him and some whispered to him softly. Some threatened him, some offered bribes. Hagurosan was terrified and confused by the attention, but all he could do was tell the truth, and so he did.

After all this, the oldest priest who had not yet spoken stood and cleared his throat. The other priests fell silent.

"This boy has been blessed with punishment," the old priest said. "The spirits have asked him to collect the coins in order to grant the wish he made. Hagurosan asked them to bless the children of the world, to help and protect those in need. The spirits have granted this wish. They are giving us the means to help the children ourselves." He looked at Hagurosan. "The coins are for the children. Hagurosan will collect them, then we will take them and spend them on children who need help."

"But it is forbidden to take offerings from the shrine," another priest said.

"Yes," the old priest agreed. "But the coins are not our offerings to the spirits. They are the offerings that the spirits have made to us."

The old priest looked at Hagurosan. His eyes were dark and deep, and Hagurosan found that he could not look away.

"You do not have to do this," the old priest said. "The spirits did not order you to stay. They only said they wanted you to collect the coins. If you choose to leave, they will not harm you. But there will be no more coins, and the children you wished to help will suffer."

Hagurosan almost fled when he heard that. He hadn't really thought about what he was saying when he made the wish, and he had no desire to give up his own freedom to help others. But now that he thought about the priest's words, he saw how much of a difference he could make. War and disease were common in his part of the world. There were many orphans, alone and helpless, doomed to die of hunger and lack of care. Now Hagurosan had the power to help them. If he turned his back on this chance, he would feel like the most miserable person on the face of the planet.

"OK," Hagurosan said, with a heavy heart and tears in his eyes. "I'll stay." And as he said it, he imagined a prison door clanging shut behind him, cutting him off from the world for the rest of his life.

No Matter the Creeds of Man
Respect the Holy
And the world is your reward

Chapter 6

Lost and Found

"*You're* the green-tooth monster!" shouted a young boy, and slapped Hagurosan hard. Hagurosan opened his lips to show his teeth, grunted like a monster, and lumbered after the children. The children ran away from him, shrieking with laughter.

Hagurosan was a young man now. Other men his age were hunting and farming, travelling to market to trade their goods, making plans to marry. But Hagurosan still stayed in the shrine. He heard from the children and other visitors about the great world outside, but he was unable to set foot in it.

He knew every last inch of the shrine. He had walked around it thousands of times. He knew every crack in every statue. He knew the birds, foxes and squirrels that came to feed on the offerings left for the spirits. They had been afraid of him to begin with, but now they saw him as just another part of the shrine.

The village at the foot of the Holy Mountain had changed beyond recognition, the visitors told Hagurosan. The coins he collected had been spent well. Shelters had been built for children who were victims of war or suffering. New bakeries had been established. Public baths. Playgrounds. Even a school!

The village elders always came to
Hagurosan for advice. They asked for his
opinion before any building work began. He had
been blessed by the spirits, and the villagers
did not want to offend them by somehow
offending Hagurosan.

When Hagurosan wasn't talking of plans with the elders, or collecting coins, he was most often to be found playing or talking with the children. The children loved him. Many were nervous, scared and surly when they first came to the village. Hagurosan put them all at their ease. He was able to talk with them, even if they didn't speak his language – this was another gift from the gods. He would spend ages with them when they came, and tell them about his past and the village. Over time, he would chip away at the defences they had built to keep the world out. First they learned to trust Hagurosan, and later to trust others.

In return for helping them, the children made sure Hagurosan had plenty of company. It was lonely on the Holy Mountain, but the children helped the days pass by. He could not help but be lonely at night, when he lay all alone in the small shack the villagers had built for him inside the shrine. But the days never dragged.

Sometimes Hagurosan was jealous of his young friends. His heart often hurt when he thought of the childhood he had lost. He would have given anything to be one of the children he helped – to be able to roam about the village, run where he wished, hunt with the men, trade at market, date girls.

But he was never sorry for the decision he had made. Almost every day new children arrived. Strays and waifs travelled for months on end to find a safe place to live. They crossed war zones, braved forests filled with wild animals and ghosts that could suck out a man's soul. Children with no parents and homes, children who'd been lost or abandoned, some on crutches, some who could only crawl. They were all hurting in one way or another. They were lost, afraid of the world, looking out on it with haunted, distrustful eyes.

Before, these children would have died, or grown up into horrid adults, filled with hate and twisted by bitterness and lack of love. Now they had a corner of the world to call their own. They had homes, food, clothes, education and love. They played with the children of the village and grew happy and strong. Smiles replaced tears and hope replaced fears.

Whenever Hagurosan felt sad or jealous, he looked into the eyes of the rescued children.

When he saw the relief and happiness there, he knew with all his heart that he had made the right decision. That didn't make the regrets go away, but it allowed Hagurosan to live with them.

Those who would take
Are those we should not trust,
As they would take all and still want more

Chapter 7

Important Priests

One day, a new group of priests climbed the Holy Mountain. They said they had come to take Hagurosan away.

"We have been sent by a prince from the far north," the head priest told Hagurosan. "He wishes to take you to live in his palace. He will use the coins to build new temples to his own spirits."

"But what about the children?" Hagurosan cried. "The spirits give me the coins to help the children."

"No," the head priest said. "We believe that the other priests did not understand the spirits' message. The spirits want us to honour them. They would not waste such a fortune on simple children."

"But they're not wasting it!" Hagurosan said.

"You are a peasant," the priest laughed. "What makes you think you know more than us? We have devoted our lives to understanding the ways of the spirits and making sense of their wishes."

"But – " Hagurosan began.

"Come!" the priest snapped. "Do not argue. Leave with us now or else – "

"It is not for you to understand the ways of the spirits," a voice broke in. It was the voice that was all voices. Hagurosan had heard it before, and he smiled. But the priests had never heard it, and they cowered in fear. "The people we speak to hear us in their hearts and have no need of interpreters," the voice that was all voices said. "Hagurosan is doing our work. Let him be, and never again claim to know our thoughts."

The voice that was all voices fell silent. Moments later the priests fled, pale and shaken. They never returned, but word spread of what had happened. In the years to come more and more people came to the Holy Mountain, to learn from the man who had heard the spirits with his heart. Hagurosan had only one thing to teach them, since there was only one thing he knew:

"Be kind to the children, and protect them," he would say with a shrug and a smile.

The people who came to see him sometimes went away wishing he had given them more advice. But when they wandered through the village of happy, warm-hearted children, they came to see that the one thing Hagurosan knew was enough. If they could get that right, everything else would one day follow.

Never doubt the glorious
It reveals itself
As time rids our souls of flesh

Chapter 8

The Voice that was All Voices Speaks Again

Many years passed. Hagurosan's parents died, and so did his friends. Hagurosan became an elder, one of the oldest ever known. He moved slowly now, and creaked when he bent to pick up the coins. He did not need to sleep much at night, or eat much.

Hagurosan enjoyed this time in his life. Every morning he would wake early and collect coins. Just after dawn, children from the town started to arrive and Hagurosan would pass the day talking and playing with them.

Hagurosan never grew tired of the children. Adults came to see him, too, and he talked with them politely, but he preferred the company of children. Perhaps he had never really grown out of his own childhood. In some ways he had been robbed of it. He had not grown up in the same way as other children, learning the ways of adults. Inside he was still a boy, and he saw the world through the fresh, hungry, curious eyes of a child.

Nobody knew how many children had been helped by Hagurosan's coins. Thousands, that was sure. Tens of thousands, it might have been. Perhaps even more. They had come from all corners of the world, had braved the harshest journeys, to find friends and protectors, comfort and rest. They were safe here. The village had grown over the years and become one of the biggest towns in the land. It had also become a haven. No tribes attacked Hagurosan's people, or made claims on the area. It was a holy place, respected by all, where children could play and grow. No war, no suffering, no hatred, no greed. There was enough for all, and all had an equal share.

As the children grew, some married and stayed in the town. Some moved away to lead happy lives in other places. Others left on a mission. They walked from town to town, village to village, and told the story of Hagurosan. They planted the seeds of an idea in the minds of the people who heard them. "This does not have to be a one-off," they said. "Children from all over the world have come together and created a heaven on earth. If that can happen in one village, why not in all?"

Hagurosan didn't think the world was ready for the message. He thought people had a long way to go before they were ready to think that they had the power to create a perfect world. But it was a start. People would grow and learn, as the children of the town grew and learned. Perhaps, many years in the future, all villages and towns would be like Hagurosan's. There would be no war, and no child or person would ever suffer or be hungry or lonely again.

One day Hagurosan was talking with some of his many children. They were telling him the latest news from the town. He always liked to hear about the town, even though he often felt a pang of envy and wished he too could walk the streets and see the place he had helped to make. But the pang was a small one, and he had learned to ignore it over the years.

Today, however, as the children were speaking, a sharp pain shot through his chest. He was surprised by it, and upset at himself for being so foolish. To shake off the feeling, he walked towards the exit, where he could pick up some coins. But when he got to the spot where the coins appeared, there was nothing. He stopped, confused, then took a few paces forward in case he had stopped at the wrong spot. Still no coin.

Hagurosan turned to ask the children if they had played a trick on him. But what he saw made the words die on his lips. The children were gathered around the body of a man by the large statue in the centre of the shrine. It was clear that the man was dead.

That man was Hagurosan.

As Hagurosan watched, the children wept and stroked the hair and face of the dead man. Two of them ran down the Holy Mountain to get help. The rest stayed to keep Hagurosan's body company.

"Can I leave now?" Hagurosan asked. His words were softer than a spring breeze.

"**Yes**," said the voice that was all voices.

"Where will I go?" Hagurosan asked.

"**Follow the path**," the voice that was all voices said. "**You will find your way. And, Hagurosan**," it added as he turned to leave, "**childhood is the purest state. The pure of heart never leave it behind. Their life takes them along a road away from it, but in the end they find their way back.**"

Hagurosan didn't understand, but he sensed that the voice that was all voices had finished. He bowed once to the statue at the centre of the shrine and gazed one last time at his own face – he hadn't realised he was *that* wrinkly! Then he left the shrine at a quick pace, keen to see what the world was like.

Mourn for what you lose
But not for long
Since all will be found if you walk in love

Chapter 9

A New World

Hagurosan walked down the Holy Mountain at a brisk trot, free now from the pains of old age. He passed through a huge, sprawling, modern town that looked nothing like the village where he had once lived. What impressed him most wasn't the new buildings, the fine roads, the schools and the playgrounds. What he loved was the look of joy and happiness on the faces of the people. They had no more riches than the people in most other towns, since all the money Hagurosan raised had gone to feeding and helping the children. But they were richer in spirit, and

Hagurosan could now see that that was the most important gift of all.

As Hagurosan left the town, the path and the countryside changed. He found himself in a new world. It was much like the one he had left, but brighter and lighter. He sensed that this world could be peaceful if he wished it to be, or full of life. It could be loud or still, vast or tiny. Anything was possible now, and it always would be.

As Hagurosan walked, he felt his body change from the body of an old, old man to the body of a child. It happened fast, in less than the blink of an eye. He stood and stared at his tiny hands and little feet. Then someone shouted his name. A young girl raced towards him, laughing and clapping. Other children followed, boys and girls, all as happy to see him as the girl in front.

Hagurosan was confused for just a second. Then he knew who the girl was – his mother.

And behind her he saw his father and his other relatives, and friends from both his childhood and his old age. And he knew them all, even though they were all now children.

As Hagurosan's mother hugged him, and the other children stood round him, he was filled with understanding of this new world.

This was what the voice that was all voices had tried to tell him. Childhood is the purest state, and the pure of heart always return to it. Life might be hard, and a person might suffer with many trials. But always, at the end, there is the promise of a return to childhood – a world of wonder, where every day is an adventure and every night is filled with splendid, endless dreams.

When he understood, Hagurosan laughed and hugged the children around him with a new joy. He had lost nothing in all his years in the shrine. He had not missed out on anything. The spirits had not stolen away his childhood. No one can steal a person's childhood, not in the long run.

Hagurosan's band of friends and family broke apart after a while and drifted away. They would come one-by-one to speak with Hagurosan later. They did not need to tire him now. There was no rush in this world.

Hagurosan's mother held his hand tight and smiled. "Are you ready for this?" she asked.

"Yes," he said.

"Then let's go!" she whooped, and ran with Hagurosan down to where the children were playing and would continue to play, in peace, security and love, for all the circles of time and the endless loops beyond.

All of the author's proceeds for this book are being donated to:

No Strings International

No Strings makes entertaining puppet films for children living in dangerous parts of the world, with special life-saving messages that teach them valuable lessons in staying safe and well. Working with the makers of the original *Muppet Show* and *Fraggle Rock*, No Strings' films are enjoyed by hundreds of thousands of children in countries like Afghanistan, Haiti, the Philippines, Indonesia, and parts of sub-Saharan Africa, where young people live with daily threats from landmines, cramped and impoverished living conditions, natural disasters, and diseases such as HIV. No Strings also trains teachers and care workers in how to use puppetry with children to explore the films' messages, so that they can act out situations together that help them learn how to be more aware and better prepared. No Strings is taking on new projects regularly, and because of people like you who support our work through buying this book, is able to reach an ever-growing number of children.

Thank You

If you would like to learn more, please visit
www.nostrings.org.uk

Our books are tested
for children and young people by
children and young people.

Thanks to everyone who consulted on
a manuscript for their time and effort in
helping us to make our books better
for our readers.